AF430169

Sunny Thoughts for Salty Souls

Sunny Thoughts For Salty Souls
Copyright © 2022 by Rebekah Steen

Photography by Rebekah Steen
Illustrations by Rebekah Steen
Cover and Interior Design by Rebekah Steen

First paperback edition 2022

All poems, photographs and illustrations originally appeared
on goldfishkiss.com or @goldfish_kiss instagram between 2010
and 2022, and have been reformatted for this book.

ISBN 979-8-218-10385-9

Sunny Thoughts for Salty Souls

Poems Thoughts and Photos

Rebekah Steen

who is ...
thinking. Who sweats
ocean and leaves a t...
of sand wherever sh...
the girl who always sh...
with wet hair, yet still look...
DARN GOOD. She's not s...
he kisses the sun. She gr...
roses before she was e...
new one. The girl with
cool scars + TAN LINES, W...
fraid to laugh LOUD.
WAYS seems to smell li...
VACATION and has more p...
STAMPS than shoes. She'...
osser + a FIGHTER, and ca...
much, without saying a word

If a swim in the ocean, walk in the sand, or hug
from nature stirs up something deep in your soul,
this collection of poems and thoughts might be
rather relatable.

If you've ever felt a connection to a beach, a
body of water, or trail, don't like missing a
sunset, and love the smell of fresh air, you
might like it too.

Or if you simply want a book to pick up that feels
like you found the journal of that cool aunt who
drives an old Bronco, knows the lyrics to every
Bob Marley song, has a smile that consumes her
face, and has some great travel stories to tell,
this might be it.

Basically, if you have some sunny, whimsical
thoughts from time to time, but also a bit of a
retrospective and salty soul...here you go and
cheers to you.

Love,

Rebekah

For Levi,
who helps
everything make
more sense.

Summer
Thoughts
Salt
Souls

This book isn't perfect, and I don't think it was really ever meant to be. One might say it's a bit all over the place. Probably because it's filled up with many memories from the past decade that included some stellar moments, heartbreak, lots of trying to make sense of things, life changes, tears, and bliss. However, when I go back and read each page, I can remember where I was and how I felt at that time. The same goes for the photos. They might seem simple, but man oh man, there is a lovely story behind each one. So, it was about time they were all compiled into something tangible (before they get lost in the abyss and noise of the digital world), to pick up, flip through, and hopefully get a good word hug or "insert self here" escape on any given day. Who knows, it'd be pretty darn sweet if something in here happens to stir up some memories of your own, too. Enjoy.

Hello sunshine
hello moon
hello all you beaches
I am so darn thankfaul for you.

IF YOU ASK ME

If you ask me what my dreams are,
my mind draws a blank
I prefer to dream with my eyes wide open
it gives my eyes room to think.
If you ask me what I'm craving,
I'd say hefty dose of soul food
you know, salt, sun, sand and fresh air
throw in a rainy day run too.
If you ask me where I'm going
I'd say I haven't a single clue
I've never known, never will,
think roads are crazy, and prefer if I flew.
If you ask me what I do
just be prepared to hear me laugh
a single noun or adjective
oh man, we're all so much more than that.
If you ask me what I regret,
it might make me cry
why take time to stir up those memories
you forgave or forget and chose to let fly.
If you asked me what I love,
hopefully you could see my heart smile
since only a few things occupy that acreage
that make each breath worthwhile.

So maybe stop asking questions for a bit
and just sit and be with me
then together we can dance with the thought
of how lovely being in a moment can be.

If love is shelter,
then I'll take a walk in the rain,
stretch my arms out wide,
and dance until I feel alive again.
Maybe write a song
where the drops are the beat,
keep the lyrics in my head
and then tap along with my feet.

There's such a wondrous
feeling of freedom
when you stop trying
to be perfect
And embrace the fountain
of priceless knowledge
known as making a mess,
Being a mess, falling
flat on your face,
and realizing the
kick ass gorgeousness
of getting back up and
trying again.

I'm over being realistic.
I want my own expanse of space
where I can see stories in shooting stars
be covered in paint
create a life that's art
and dance all over the place.

LETTING GO

I picked up a seashell
and threw it back to the sea
because after all
that's where it loves to be.
A drop of rain fell on my cheek
and rolled down to my lips
so I blew a kiss to the sky
figuring the drop would be missed.
There was a flower behind my ear
that someone I loved picked for me
so I let it fall to the ground
where it's colors needed to be seen.
I'm learning there's so much to take
but if you do, it just ends at that.
I suppose when you can give it away
it writes a love story right back.
So I think I'll keep on walking
and adoring simple things I pass by.
They just show the joy of loving
learning to let go
and figuring out why.

A kiss from
the sun
is a hug
for the soul

I went for a walk
kicked off my shoes,
picked a few flowers
and forgot all the news.
Sculpted notes in some clouds
let myself laugh,
rolled out a cozy blanket
and soaked up a nap.

INSPIRE ME

I just am in need of some true inspiration
and all I see are blurred perfect faces
dozens of words saying the same sort of thing
and pictures of dreamy hued places.
So I think I'll go for a walk or a drive
and think about what really sparks me within
get out of my head and into fresh air
Yup. Sounds like a good place to begin.
Maybe dance to a favorite song on repeat
close my eyes to paint murals in my dreams
create, mistake, and create some more
without fear of it ever being seen.
I'll drink up a few more sunrises
stay up way too late to write down what I think.
Be motivated by my own damn sweat
and stare at the ocean until I forget to blink.
You see, that stuff gives a brain butterflies
and an internal smirky ambition that can't be seen.
I'm just learning when it comes to true inspiration
you'll rarely find it on a screen.

MAY
YOU
NEVER
BE
TOO
BUSY
TO
STOP
and
BREATHE
UNDER
a
COCONUT
TREE.

Out here living
a fresh air loving
colorful and
not too serious
but seriously finding
the beauty in everyday
kinda life.

I'd rather be adorned in flowers
and covered in sand
where no one knows me
and I can't think of a plan.
I prefer beat up old cutoffs
and a worn out tee,
with a bit of a sunburn
and a view of the sea.
I'd choose a simpler life,
as long as it has a view,
where I listen to the birds
as the breeze sings to you.

Sunsets that never seem to fade
and a good long juicy kiss
inspiration found on rainy nights
and some belly laugh bliss.
That favorite song on repeat
and stormy morning coffees
fights that turned into bear hugs
and finding some old torn up jeans.
Feeling the sand between my toes
and alarm clock pup kisses
catching a glance that melts my heart
and therapeutic cries I didn't know existed.
Sleepless nights watching starry skies
and having something to say
then letting it all out.
You know, it's all of those moments
rarely found on a to-do list
that are what it's all about.

I'm just a son of a beach
who gives the sky a wave
chooses laughs over likes
and treads water most days.
I keep it salty yet sweet
asks the sea, shell we dance,
knows there's no place like nowhere
and gives bliss a chance.

Put a flower in your hair
as a reminder
that all it takes
is a kiss from Mother Nature
to feel beautiful
and realize
how much you still can bloom.

No inspirational quote
no motivational speech
just need a hand to hold
a reason to laugh
a deep breath
and permission to see
where life takes me.
No guilt for what I'm lacking
no shame for my missteps
just need a hefty dose of grace
and the love from a God
who embraces my humanness.

When asked what I do for a living,
I'm going to say...

I'm a dreamer,
a glassy wave seeker, an art maker
and a passport stamp collector.
I have a masters and laughter,
and am a world renown mess maker.
I'm a wannabe world changer,
a frequent smiler,
a devoted pray-er,
and an avid forgiver.
I'm a sand magnet and sun seeker,
an accident prone adventurer,
and hopefully, when I look back,
a professional life-rider
and full fledged compassion giver.

I know that's a long introduction,
and it would look weird on a résumé.
But it's what I'm doing,
when I feel like my life
is one that's really living.

I've fallen in
Love with The
Sounds of
a Warm ad
Sunny morning

Had a lovely day in the sea and sand,
although I didn't get much done.
Watched coconut tree shadows
dance across the land,
and ended up getting too much sun.
Tried to read a book I brought,
but went for a swim instead,
and I ended up simply floating along
while humming a happy tune
that was stuck in my head.
Was going to go for a run,
but I just sat and stared at the view.
Was covered in sand,
juggling shells in my hands
and thankfully realized
soaking up being at the beach
is pretty darn productive too.

Bathe in the sunshine
snuggle with the sea,
write thoughts in the sand
what a glorious day that would be.

I sat in a hammock
under the coconut trees,
sang with the birds
and dreamed of the breeze.
The tide came up
so I dipped one foot in,
hummed some Bob Marley
then dozed off
with my thoughts again.

Isn't it ironic
how the ocean
can clear your
mind and also
fill it up with
ideas at the
same time.

Leaving a place you love
is just a different kind of heartbreak
that deepens each time you say goodbye,
not knowing if your heart
will ever feel at home again
for more than a few days at a time.

Please give my heart
the sound of silence
the feeling of open space
the taste of sunshine
the scent of simplicity
and the sight of joy's embrace.

Peace of mind
is just a
breezy Beach
Walk Away

There's some
comfort in
sleepless nights
When you look up at
The stars and know
Someone, somewhere
has the same worries
Singing a song
on Repeat.

Thank you sunshine,
thank you sea,
thank you forest,
and thank you breeze.
Thank you summits,
thank you valleys,
and those wide open spaces
as far as I can see.
I'm forever filled with gratitude
for how you make me feel better
without ever speaking
a single word to me.

SUNSHINE
ON MY MIND
EVEN WHEN
it's HARD
TO FIND

You're such a beach
who shines like the sun
thinks life's such a peach
kisses the sky, then runs.
You know time grows wings
and flies down the runway
so you juice that sucker up.
Carpe diem. Seize the day.
You're the salt of the earth
that tangos with the sea
laughs through thunderstorms
and inspires as you breathe.

She searches
for seashells
by the seashore
and gets lost
in her thoughts
as she keeps on
looking for more.

Warm sand says
welcome home to my feet,
and my tears like
to stay with the sea.
Seashells often
hold my hand,
and my hair is learning
the wind's choreography.

I Like to
say hello
to the Sea
because it
always
waves
back to Me.

Sometimes the heartbreak
wells up so deep inside,
that the only place
it can overflow
is in the ocean.
But when the sea isn't close,
it just creates waves
in my soul,
and the tides run down my face
one drop at a time.

HELLO OCEAN

Hello ocean, my old friend
I'm learning I'm more like you again.
We have our high tides,
we have our lows
Those vulnerable depths
where broken beauty grows.
You have warm breezes,
and I take deep breaths
both somehow cleanse my mind
until there's no worries left.
We have our waves,
some are gentle, some are rough
they're baby steps each day
that vanish and say good luck.
You have your depths,
I have thoughts only I know
few people will dive deep
to understand those lows.
We have our surface,
we have our currents
those impossible parts of us
that make little sense.
You splash, I crash,
we have riptides and storms
then wake up to sunlit glassy mornings,
our favorite art form.
You have your saltwater, and I do too
maybe that's why it's such a relief
to always cry with you.

So if I come back frequently,
to hold my breath and dive on in,
Just please continue to wrap me
in your salty, loving,
I totally understand you, arms
...time and time again.

Life is a
mystery
and
no one has
it figured out.
Some People
just enjoy
it More.

Went for a swim in the sea
to soak up its peace,
and a school of fish
came to dance along side me.
We dove down to the depths
to glide on the sand,
tracing remnants of waves
with their fins and my hand.
We flipped and we twirled
then stared up at the sun.
Then I simply floated to freeze time,
and the magic begun.

Whenever I feel NUMB, it's a sign of needing to Dive into a Wave to have some Saltiness Slapped back into Me.

There is a sublime magic
in the ocean's ability
to play the exact song
I need to hear
at any given time.

When it's gray
you want sunshine,
and when it's sunny
you crave the rain.
Or maybe it's that
we all get pretty antsy
when things just
stay the same.

Baby it's
cold outside,
but it's 72
and balmy in
my mind.

How do you thank a sunset
for its soothing song of hues,
or write the forest a love song
for its innumerable inspiring tunes.
If only I could give a cloud a hug
and we could dance through open spaces
whispering about all the times
they took my mind to happier places.
I'd write a poem to the sea
about how its waves calmed my breaths
and one to the views on my favorite hike
for soaking up worries until I had none left.
I guess that's the gorgeousness of nature
it gives us exactly what we need
without expecting anything in return.
So maybe to show my gratitude
I need to come back frequently
but leave it as it is, and always learn.

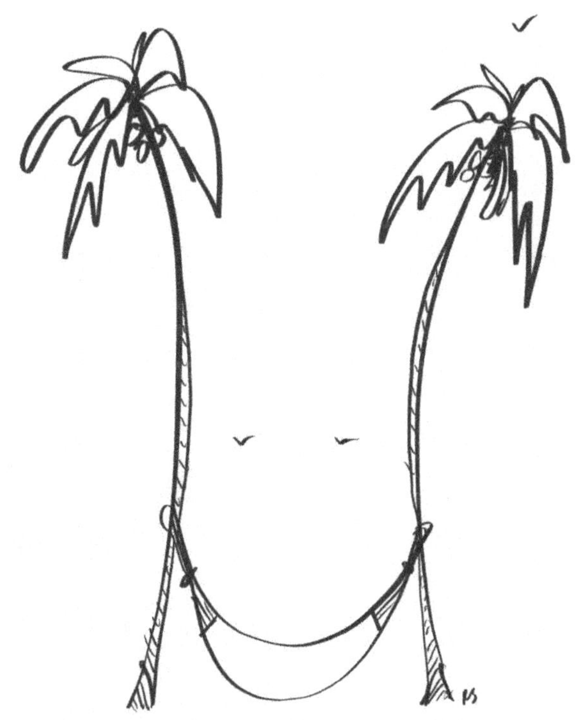

TAKE A WHILE TO JUST
THINK OF SOMETHING
THAT MAKES YOU SMILE.

Dear Nature,
Thanks for making me feel tiny, powerless,
and yet refreshed and like a total badass
all at once.

THAT PLACE

You know that place,
that you dream of while dreaming.
Where you'll gladly get up at 5 am
just to be there to watch it wake up.
The sight of it gives you permagrin,
and the thought of leaving makes you tear up.
That place where the breeze
reminds you to breathe,
the waves whisper your worries away,
you make out with the sun,
and the water blends perfectly
with your tears.
You need nothing but a way to get there,
want nothing but to live there,
and would give everything
so it would never change.
It gets you, yet it always
leaves you guessing.
You've told it your thoughts,
and it answered in a sunset.
And when it comes down to it,
it's just so damn beautiful
that adjectives rarely do it justice.
You know that place that seems to hug, love,
and understand you in ways no human can?

Go there.
As much as possible.
And dream of it when you're away.

Things haven't really
gone according to plan,
but it's all turning out
to be more beautiful
than I could've ever imagined.

I've decided to stop trying
to figure out what God is doing,
because I'll never understand.
So I wake up each day and give thanks
for what's in store for me.
But hope one day it will be to live
where I wake up and feel the sand.

I sold everything
and found an old truck,
packed a few dreams
and wished the sky luck.
Cranked up some good tunes
and sang to the views,
then I found the sea
and my eyes hugged its hues.
Kicked off my shoes
to dance in the waves,
and cried happy tears
'cause I knew this was the place.

I'm not really a mermaid.
I'm just a gal
who loves the water
and has to come up for air
from time to time.

The thought of
walking barefoot
in the sand
each day makes
me want to fly
somewhere
far
far away.

Not a single person who has walked on this
beautiful Earth has been able to please
everyone, yet for some reason I still try
to be the first, and it's exhausting.

Sometimes my heart breaks
into a puzzle,
but leaves a missing piece
that I hope helps
complete a beautiful image
in someone else's life.

Went for walk on a rainy day,
but I kept on looking down.
Watched the drops tap the puddles
to spread their song around.
Saw a single flower floating
and twirling to the weather's beat.
Then realized all this
took the noise that was in my brain
and somehow pressed delete.

It aint
all butterflies
and rainbows

but it's pretty
nice when it is.

She's not
sunkissed,
she kisses
the sun

THAT GIRL

You know that girl,
the one who is always smiling or thinking,
who sweats the ocean
and leaves a trail of sand
behind her wherever she goes.
The girl who always shows up with wet hair,
yet still looks so darn good.
She's not sun kissed, she kisses the sun.
She grew her own flowers
before she was ever given one.
The girl with the cool scars & tan lines,
who isn't afraid to laugh loud.
She always seems to smell like vacation
and has more passport stamps than shoes.
She's a hugger and a fighter,
and can say so much,
without saying a word.

You know that girl you always wanted to be?

Be her.

No tutorial, beauty product, or filter can
ever recreate the glow of badass joy filled
gorgeousness that a woman feels when walking
out of the ocean.

You're the pot
of GOLD
at the end of
THE RAINBOW,
And you don't
even know
IT, BABY :)

There are some things you miss so much
you end up trying to forget them.
Then one day you see or feel something
and it reminds you of those missed
and attempted to forget things.
But, it feels like hope
wrapped up in a bear hug,
because it helped you realize
what you've missed has been with you,
helped make you who you are today,
and will always be with you,
in some shape, feeling or form.

The weather is my DJ
the wildflowers are my crowd
the fresh air is my shelter
and starry skies are my town.

when
I Look
up at a
coconut tree
sometimes I
think it's
reaching out
to hug me.

I like to party.
And when I say party
I mean lay on the sand
with a coocnut in my hand
and no one else is in sight.

ONE DAY

She was in a certain season
and felt a bit out of place
knew everything happens for a reason
but still stared heartbreak in its face.
Days felt like a skipping record
and self care meant remembering to floss
thankfully joy made frequent appearances
reminding her purpose was not lost.
Spontaneous ugly cries happened
same with moments of bliss
and part of her often wondered
if she could give a nap a kiss.
She knew to keep on going
with her head aimed towards the sky
searching for paradise in the grayness
loving each day then letting it fly.
It's like she walked out the door barefoot
down a long sandy road of regime
wandering aimlessly and hoping
to one day figure out her dream.

The sun has kissed my skin so much it's left a
splattering of love letters on my cheeks, a map
for tears to find my smile, and parched lips
that are only quenched by a dip in the sea.

BELLE

Her mirror isn't made of glass
can't be broken, cleaned or smeared.
She'd rather see her reflection in a laugh
because it's lovelier when heard.
She'd prefer to stare at a flower
and ask, what do you think of me?
then pick it, put it behind her ear
and have it whisper as she sings.
She'll wake up with the sun
and have it bathe her tired face,
it will kiss her no matter what
leaving love letters she can't erase.
She'll stop to look at her reflection
in a puddle after the rain,
then smash it with her foot and smile
and dance in some drops again.
Or sometimes she'll just go for a walk
and take a juicy deep breath,
then the wind will whistle a cat call
that puts some extra pep in her step.
Yes, she knows she's gorgeous,
but not in your typical,
on the surface, way.
She just learned that when she loves life
it'll tell her that she's beautiful.

Always.

sunkissed

just let me
lay in the sand
and paint
paradise in
the clouds

You're always enough
for a hug from a tree,
a love song from the birds,
and a dance with the sea.

I go on a run to get away from my thoughts,
a hike to find a better view,
hop in for a swim to catch my breath,
and dance around to feel brand new.

RICH

I might not be able to buy a home these days
but I've made dozens of castles in the sand.
My car's always a mess and needs some repairs
but I've walked barefoot in the rain holding hands.
I don't get invited to fancy parties
that are smothered in shimmering lights.
But I've caught jars full of fireflies
on humid starry summer nights.
I've jumped off a boat in quite a few seas
smiled and hugged in languages I don't know.
Watched sunsets that sang me symphonies
and soaked up laughs when time feels slow.
It's those priceless feeling and memories
that I want to think of, hold onto and thank.
Because even if I'm never a millionaire
I'm getting rich in ways that don't count at the bank.

Time flies,
but you are the
Pilot. So remember
to LAND in
Places that
Make you feel
Like Sunshine.

I love listening to conversations
in languages I don't know
while still understanding
the laughter of friends
telling stories of a joy filled life.

Rebekah Steen

It feels good to feel good, but it also
feels good to cry, scream, and give that
hurricane that's been brewing in my soul
some time to rage.

NATURAL BEAUTY

She looked in the mirror
and finally saw something different.
It's almost like it was a window
into times well spent.
She saw eyes that listened to the ocean
and learned to smile back.
Lips that kissed the sky
and concealed a notorious laugh.
Cheeks painted by endless summers
with freckles that spelled out job well done.
Hair that was as wild as her spirit
and the best dance partner the wind had known.
A smile that illuminated her face
and revealed sun-bleached teeth.
Imperfect yet glowing skin
that drank up fresh air
and thought sweat, tears, and rain
tasted oh so sweet.
She embraced this lovely new perspective
and went outside for a while,
picked a flower to go behind her ear
looked up, took a breath...and smiled.

home
is where
the SANDY
toes PLAY
AND
THE
Palm TREES
SWAY.

Picked a flower for my hair
and started to run,
got smothered in ideas
and played tag with the sun.
Typed thoughts in my brain
and painted dreams of my own
...then forgot it all
when I picked up my phone.

HOME SWEET HOME

My home may never be perfect, or worthy of a
magazine, but it will be a blessed mess where
a pot of coffee is always brewing, cold beers
are waiting in the fridge, the kitchen doubles
as a dance floor, sandy feet are more than
welcome, and pups are encouraged to cuddle with
you anywhere. It will remind you of the beach,
make you smile, want to curl up somewhere and
kick up your feet, or bust open a bottle of wine
and stay a while. There might be dust, dirt,
and unorganized chaos, but there will be even
more laughter, hugs, cooking and creative mess
making. I'll try and keep it clean, but will try
even harder to make sure it welcomes people with
cozy open arms. There will be too many pillows,
some stuff that reminds me of a college dorm,
a ton of flowers, plants I'll attempt to keep
alive, and cute little hand prints on windows
that I don't want to wash off. It'll just be
home. Wherever it is. Our sweet, full of love
and aloha, home.

I don't know where home is
but I know where my heart is,
and it's broken into pieces
then scattered across the globe
with my dreams as the treasure map
to go out and find them.

Sometimes the best cure
is a horizon to stare at
a blanket
a few deep breaths
and a good cup of coffee.

Each day is a blank page, waiting for a
poem. So swap the to-dos for some prose,
live a little, and let your mind roam.
Each life is a canvas, that no one has
figured out. So make a mess, use up all
the colors, spare the critiques, and
embrace what each brush stroke's about.

What a wondrous feeling it is
to watch the sun wake up the world
and then tuck it in to sleep
on the same day.

Remember to
Press Pause
and go Look
at The STARS
wow
hi
missed ya
ahhh

It's not escaping reality, it's just making reality be pretty dreamy for a few days.

I just want
to surf underneath
a full moon
and watch its reflections
tell the waves
about everything
it's seen
over the past month.

Never waste the inspiration of a rainy night
when the drops sing your dreams love songs
and your brain gets butterflies.
It's a present unwrapped by the clouds
begging you to breathe, mute the worries,
and soak up nature's symphony.

Have you ever thanked the moon
for reminding you there's sunshine
on the darkest nights,
or smiled at the stars
for splatter painting a symphony
in silent lights.

I'm pretty certain
the phase of the moon mirrors
the amount of thoughts
that fill my head
as I try to fall asleep.

The only
sunsets I don't
Like are the
ones that I miss.

LEAP

There once was a girl who took a leap of faith
she just closed her eyes and dove right in.
Then she woke up one day in the right place
and began to smile from within.
The more she dreamed the more she lived
and life started loving her right back.
She had time to enjoy the little things
like sunsets, salty air and plenty of laughs.
Sunshine followed her even when it rained
and beaches missed her toes when she left.
Yeah, she still had her off and down days
but would find joy even retracing her steps.
So she simply decided to keep on this track
of taking leaps and often swimming upstream.
To blindly move forward, and rarely look back
and follow, or at least jump, into a dream.

Please let the sun shine on my face
so that sun spots create constellations
to guide me back to my happy place.

her hand. A Deep Salt
breath relaxed her lungs.
Clearing out space where
nxiety hung. Birds chirped gre
to Sing her Blues away.
Warm cozy breezes knew
just what to say. Those
arry Nights in WIDE open sp
danced with her dreams
to wander New Plac
lear Water on her skin
erased any self D
And the Wildflowers
they were HER TYPE of

—Rebekah Steen
(Costa Rica 2019)

Nature embraced her
like no one else can
she'd soak it up
and it held her hand.
A deep salty breath
relaxed her lungs
clearing out that space
where anxiety hung.
Birds chirped greetings
to sing her blues away
and cozy warm breezes
knew just what to say.
Those deep starry nights
in wide open spaces
danced with her dreams
to wander new places.
Clear water on her skin
erased any self doubt
and the wildflowers knew
they were her type of crowd.

The less I try to do
the more I accomplish
the more I appreciate
and the more I end up
living the kind of life
that feels like a sponge
soaking up the good stuff.

Hello loneliness
it's you again
but what I really wanted
was a laugh-filled
unfiltered and nonscheduled
day with some friends.

I often feel
So Lonely IN A
Crowded City,
Yet ALWAYs feel
Loved and Hugged
When Its JUST
Me And SoME
COCONUT TREES.
FREE HUGS

I feel like I've had
more than one life
but they are all
pieces to a puzzle
that will one day
come together
to make a picture
more beautiful
than I could imagine.

I know you're supposed
to keep your head up
but somedays
if you keep your head down
you see the beauty in things
often overlooked.

Oh how lovely it is
to go to bed and dream
of all the dots on a map
you want to connect
that will paint a beautiful
ever-changing picture
of adventure.

to do:
Live more
Love more

It's such a weird feeling
to be grateful
but know you're not thriving,
to take a deep breath
but wonder what it's hiding
to thank the Lord
for each day with a smile,
but have a soul
that's also crying.

When the sun wakes up and
says howdy each day
I simply roll over in bed
and pray my worries away.
I'll give em up to the sky
no mater what the burden
always thanking the Lord
'cause I know that he heard 'em.
You'd think that'd be it
that it all goes away
but oh no, worry still seeps in
in its own sneaky way.
But that's just how it goes
rituals with breaths of grace
simple steps that help in finding
some peace in this crazy place.

faith

She always admires the sunset
looks up at the stars as they take a bow.
She gets lost in the desert
following it's hues wherever it allows.
She'd kiss every cloud if she could
just to have their dreams touch her face.
She could sit at a beach for hours
breathing the beauty of the place.
Misty mornings leave her speechless
and mountains hug her with their views.
Hopefully one day she'll look at herself
and see she's also a stunning creation
that's totally worth admiring, too.

There's beauty in every day...
some days take more effort
in finding it,
and some days you might
have to close your eyes.
Often times it will slap you
right in the face,
or sometimes
it's looking back at you
and takes you by suprise.

"How's your day"
I get asked once in a while,
but to give the true answer
would take an hour to explain,
so I just say, "Good"
with a half ass smile.

If you are failing,
falling or feeling awkward
and your comfort zone
is out of site
take a deep breath
and learn to laugh at it all
because everything's
gonna be alright.
The sweat, tears,
and harshness of falls
are craving a lovely embrace.
It's all a side effect
of growing, learning and living.
Plus, it'd be so boring
if things only fell
perfectly in place.

All I'm hoping, praying and trying to do, is live my life in a way where I never have to look back to find the best of times.

RS

I might never write a book,
but I have a shelf that's
filled with dusty travel journals
overflowing with stories
only I can tell.

To all the
tears, wipeouts
and every closed door.
The embarassing moments
calls that never rang
and jobs I didnt get.
The mean people
crazy bosses
and egomaniacs.
All the falls, trips
dents and dings.
The sunburns, scratches
sweat and soreness.
The missed opportunities
missed flights, lost bags
and empty tanks of gas.
All the breakups, hangups
and unanswered prayers.

I thank you,
from the bottom of my heart
for shaping me into what I am today.

Don't mind me,
I just need to Dream
of living on my own
Private Island
for a few minutes.

she didn't fear
too many things,
other than a life
that felt like
someone pressed
the repeat button
and her song
was muted.

I might never actually know what I want to be,
but I know I want to be known as the person
who made you laugh, who said hell yeah to
adventures, sunset sessions, going barefoot,
guac, fresh air and dessert. Who asked you about
you, got up and danced, jumped in and swam, and
closed her eyes to take that leap of faith. The
gal who loved flowers, wore flowers, bought
flowers and always smelled like them too. Who
dared, fell, lost, cuddled, cried, soaked up as
many moments as possible, got down and dirty,
forgave like a champ, and was a kick ass total
rockstar of a person to be around. I want to be
the gal who lived, lived some more, loved even
more, threw her head back, laughed, and was a
child at heart up until the very end.

So maybe, afterall, I really just want to be,
and be known as...the best me I knew how to be.

If you see me kicking off my shoes
and smiling at my leathery feet
I'm reminiscing and craving some time
of dancing barefoot at the beach.

I want to travel the world, and live out of
a backpack, but also want a bungalow near the
beach, always knowing where my home's at. I
want to live on a boat, and sail the azul seas,
but also want to wake up and feel grounded,
maybe have some sort of routine. But, if I take
a step back and stop to think while I breathe,
I might realize those dreams could happen at
some point, but right now all that I have is
just what I need.

H·O·L·A

A HUGE THANK YOU

...to anyone who ever told me over the years that one of these poems was exactly what you needed to hear on that very day. Or that it was as if I read your mind or something. Or that you loved my writing, and it was like talking to a friend. Life is a crazy ride, but also can be so lonely. However, there is something so special about knowing people all over the globe connect with what I'm saying or feeling, however simple or complex it may be. It's surreal but also like a big hug at the same time. Your encouragement means more than you'll ever know, and essentially, made me realize how much I needed to kick my self-doubt to the curb and create this book. It's also what keeps me loving every time I find time to write, and I am so grateful for that.

...to my husband who keeps me on my toes, and moves us all over the place which ultimately brewed up so many of the emotions that inspired these pages. Thanks for understanding my constant need to travel back to the beach, too. One day I'll write you a love poem.

...to my mom for reading everything, finding typos, and leaving me voice messages where you read the poems out loud. Thanks for telling everyone you come in contact with to check out my stuff, too.

Heb. 11.1 Faith shows the reality of what we hope for; it is the evidence of things we cannot see.

ABOUT THE AUTHOR

Rebekah Steen is an artist, writer, photographer, designer, and all-around creative gal. She is commonly known as Goldfish Kiss thanks to the name of her blog that's been around since 2008. Since you're here for writing details, she went to the University of Iowa and received her BFA in Graphic Design in 2003, but also took every single creative writing class she could without being enrolled in the Iowa Writers' Workshop the university is famous for. So, she declared herself a creative writing minor as well. She's been filling up countless notebooks ever since, and although she could write a stellar story one day, poetry's been a rather lovely fit.

She's married to her hunk of a husband, they have an awesome li'l dude, and their pup, Kili, completes the family. She currently lives in Washington but moves quite frequently so who knows where she will be once you read this. But it's a guarantee she will be dreaming of living back at the beach.

This is her first book, and an art book is coming soon. Hopefully it won't be another decade before she publishes another poetry book, because this one was one helluva fun one to create.

If any of this floats your boat, you can follow her over at goldfishkiss.com and @goldfish_kiss

(The photo is Rebekah in Pensacola Beach, Florida. Gotta love that sugar sand. Muwah.)